AEGEAN VOYAGE

AEGEAN VOYAGE

THE LIGHT AND THE SMILE

Photographs
YIORGOS DEPOLLAS

Texts
MEMOS TSELIKAS

Translation
JOHN STATHATOS

ATHENS 1996
FOTORAMA

Photographs: Yiorgos Depollas
Texts: Memos Tselikas
Publishing Manager: Alexandros Valavanis
Design: Yiorgos Depollas
Art Direction: Dimitris Korovessis
Translation: John Stathatos

Published and produced in Greece by editions FOTORAMA Co.,
52, Sina Str. GR - 106 72 Athens.
Tel.: (01) 364.3592 - FAX: (01) 364.3323

ISBN : 960-7524-02-0

CONTENTS

INTRODUCTION

*I can still remember many details
of my first 'serious' journey
to Ios, in 1970.
Since that time, and in many different
ways, I have come to know
many places in the Aegean.
It's true that I still haven't been able
to see all of them,
and I've come to love some
more than others.
The material which makes up this book
was selected from
among the photographs
taken on all my visits;
in effect, it represents a journey
begun quarter of a century ago,
and which is
still unfinished...*

Yiorgos Depollas

THE AEGEAN: FROM MYTH TO HISTORY

The ship with the black sails had come from Crete and was approaching Cape Sounion. When the king saw it, his despair was such that he flung himself into the sea and was drowned. The king was Aegeus, King of Athens, and the ship with the black sails coming up from the south was that of his son, Theseus. She was returning in triumph, for Theseus had succeeded in killing Minotaur in his labyrinth and was bringing back to Athens her young men. Their joy was such that they forgot to change the sails from black to white, the pre-arranged signal of victory. Irony, working through that splash of black, went on to consecrate this sea with the name of the dead king, and now they call it the Aegean. Those who leaf through old books will find many such myths woven around this sea. Perhaps they make up its history, because at every time and in every period, this sea with its dozens of islands seems to generate superhuman and unique myths, like the sea monsters on the margins of old charts or the gorgon which rises up from the waves to ask whether King Alexander lives. Civilisations lost in time, whose remains mark their vigour and their passing. Stone tools, small white idols in male and female shapes, jars decorated with octopus and flying fish, clay mirrors incised with circles which hark back to the palaeolithic and neolithic. The frescoes in the palaces of Thera speak of a sophisticated maritime society whose vessels knew every corner of the Mediterranean. Nor, according to Homer, were the princes of the archipelago slow to come forth when the kings of Sparta and Mycenae ventured against Troy. Names, words, activities and archaeological finds all confirm the real essence of the mythical narratives. The islanders, the men of the Aegean sea, men of life and action, created what the historians have named the Aegean Civilisation to stand alongside that of the Myceneans and Minoans.

Both Herodotus and then Thucidides, in the course of narrating the events of what by now were classical times, described the Aegean as the vital region on which rested the power of Athens and Sparta. The islands were essential stopovers for the ships which crossed the sea to the Greek colonies along all the shores of the Mediterranean, from the Black Sea in the north and Ionia in the east to Egypt in the south and the Pillars of Hercules in the west. The islands were the stepping stones and their men made up the ships' crews – men who knew the ways of stars and winds, who knew the shapes of mountains and the safest way into harbours. In this sea was born the strategic doctrine according to which control of the seas means control of the world. And it was precisely to the control of this sea that Athens owed her glory.

The history of most Aegean islands during Roman and Byzantine times is obscure for long periods. The inscriptions and ruins which archaeology is constantly bringing to light testify that these islands always played an important role in the commerce and defence of the two great empires. For as long as powerful navies ensured the freedom of the seas, there was safety and prosperity. On the contrary, when there was no organised naval presence, the islands became vulnerable to piratical raids. This resulted in the foundation of settlements whose first priority was defence. The very walls of the houses in the outer perimeter became a defensive wall, pierced by a small number of postern gates. Despite pressure from Arab and pirate raids, the Byzantine state succeeded in keeping open the Aegean sea lanes until the 12th century; however, this control was gradually eroded by the constant granting of concessions to Venice and Genoa, the Mediterranean's latest naval powers, concessions which allowed them to open commercial stations on the empire's littoral. The Fourth Crusade and the destruction of Constantinople by the Latins in 1204 resulted in a new distribution of power in the Aegean. The great islands like Chios and Mytilene passed into the control of the Genoese, Rhodes went to Knights of St. John, and the Cyclades to the Venetians, who founded the Duchy of the Archipelago. Frankish families settled in the islands and imposed a social and economic structure based on western, feudal principles until, from 1560 onwards, they fell one after the other to the Turks. For the islanders, the change of masters was of little importance, since their lives and property were no less at their mercy; but they lost nothing of their maritime soul. The sea remained their world, and they drew hope from it. Their role had been defined since ancient times: they would always be carriers of the fortunes of others. What is impressive, however, is the fact that this state of dependency never led them to develop a servile attitude; rather the opposite. In the organisation of their communities and in their activities in general they developed defensive mechanisms and dynamic initiatives. Their centre of reference now was Constantinople, known simply as The City. Taking advantage of the Turks' lack of maritime experience, they succeeded in controling a large part of the conveyancing trade within the Ottoman empire; they also acquired privileges thanks to which they became effectively self-governing within their communities. In this way they gradually grew stronger politically and financially from the 17th century onwards, so that when the war of liberation which broke out in 1821 in the Peloponnese reached them, they were not slow to revolt and gain their longed-for liberty and independence.

THE VOYAGE TO LIGHT AND SMILES

Once upon a time, travellers on their way to Greece from Europe would take ship in Venice or Marseilles and sail to the Ionian sea. If they then wanted to continue east, they first had to negotiate the three southern capes of the Peloponnese, between Kythera and Cape Maleas. Then they could choose their route: northwards for Constantinople, eastwards for Chios and Mytilene, south for Rhodes and Cyprus. Whichever they chose, they would have to wander through the Aegean, the Archipelago or White Sea as it was called. White Sea: a fortuitous naming. Perhaps it was because of the foaming waves which the north-west wind raises winter and summer, whitening the sea from end to end. Or perhaps because of the sun's bright light, which is mirrored by the water and dispersed in a thousand facets; or else again because this light can reach to the depths of your soul, filling you with joy and optimism. However that may be, the Aegean is in truth a white sea. Even today's traveller, however he may reach it, is seduced by the same invincible light. No other part of Greece has been depicted by foreign travellers as often as the Aegean. And that is because its very nature, its people, its history and the unexpected transformations of its landscape and colours inspire the imagination to weave epics and fairy tales, so that it can become impossible to distinguish between fact and fantasy.

On board the packet steamer between Tzia lighthouse and Kythnos, and across from you, at the horizon's eye, the dawn is turning the sky and the sea red. You forget yourself, the voices grow fainter and you lose yourself in a new dream, a dream carried upon the perfumed wind blowing from shore. The world all around you travels with you, as though there were just you and it. Words, names, faces you loved and love, a song's melody which rises to your lips and which you hum. It is not like being on a mountain peak, from where you can see far into the distance and feel like the master of the world. Here the world itself embraces you. A little more and you can touch the horizon. Your solitude vanishes. You too become a wave, foam, a drop of brine, a ray of the sun, a breath of wind, a small part of the world in which you live and of whose infinity and grandeur you partake. And when night falls, how many stars travel along with you. How many of the island lights seem to be hanging in the empyrean. How many lighthouse beams greet you and call you to them. Dialogue, coexistence, collaboration are immediate and unending.

The mountain ranges, the placid bays, the rocks falling down to the depths, the carnival of colours, the intoxicating perfume of the inland wild flowers, all these together and separately tempt the soul's hidden powers to emerge from the subconscious. Rocks eaten by the sea and by the wind, the grey wrinkled face of time which looks into your eyes trying to communicate the deepest sense of eternity. That rumour, the barely audible echo of waves which, driven wild by the wind, flood into underwater caves, frightens you, as though the very earth were on the verge of yawning open, about to swallow you like a dragon. And yet you do not turn your face away in fear, but rather struggle to fold this power within yourself for ever.

The approach to an island always gives rise to a sense of intangible expectation. From a distance, it seems like a shadow fallen across blue velvet. Slowly but surely, this shadow takes on colour and dimensions.

You bear off, come round the cape, and all is changed. A beach extends peacefully, caressed by the sea. Higher up, on land, one, two, three houses, small gardens, the snaking drystone walls which once separated pastures, the terraced vineyards and olive groves, a white chapel. A few small mirrors glimmer here and there: child's play, a few handfuls of sunlight collected and flung back at the ships in greeting. Light from light, the smile of people from the smile of the day. The stranger is no stranger, he is somebody we knew in another life, returned to us by time.

However much things may have changed, with so many ships travelling back and forth, when the ship of the line comes into an island harbour, the arrival becomes a celebration. Sometimes there are more people waiting outside than there are arriving. This is not out of idle curiosity, but from a deep urge to see and hear something new, to be the first to shake the hand of an acquaintance, to show that one exists. And the others, those on board, come down the gangways like victors and set foot on land in a bedlam of shouts, parcels, bundles, cars and motorcycles, their eyes scanning restlessly. Everything seems huge and excessive, until the crowd slowly settles, the ship casts loose and heads off to another harbour, until you find a bench or a chair in a cafe on which to leave the tiredness of your journey and get your second wind.

Much will seem strange to you. You had imagined something else, photographs and advertising had promised something different, this is not what your reading had led you to expect. You try to confirm or reject these expectations, but in fact what you are doing is slowly forming your own personal view, guided now by a glance, now by a smile, a word exchanged in passing, a sound, a gesture. There is much you cannot understand; some things you accept, others you reject, others provoke your curiosity. In no case, however, do you remain a disinterested observer. Just as the voyage itself had made you aware of the world's magic, you now engage in a process of discovery and participation. The measure of all is your heart. However much contemporary reality might try to codify patterns of behaviour in conformity with the chilly requirements of tourist bureaux, there is much that still escapes them and which can still, often in the most unorthodox way, give a sense of the local colour. Is this not, too, a challenge? A country bearing the traditions of thousands of years, which has seen so many invaders, which struggles to live in the world today whilst maintaining its own identity – not out of unthinking resistance to everything foreign, but to safeguard a way of life with a different understanding of human relationships – offers you the opportunity of familiarising yourself with it and of living alongside it.

Wandering through the narrow streets between the houses of the old island settlements is enough to release your mind from its usual rhythms. If your heart is open and your mood inclines you to accept the call of this unfamiliar beauty, you have already begun the process of assimilation into the mysteries of colours, forms, sounds and smells. A wall, a doorway, a window, a stone staircase, a cobbled street seem as if they too might have a soul. Irregular, unshaped stones one above the other, with nothing between them, a dry-stone wall, manage to stand harmoniously in balance, protecting a walled garden from the wind. The tops of some trees emerge bravely above it as though in emulation of the bold cypress trees which march proudly up to the sky. Even the unruly jasmine, the modest night-blooming cereus and the gay red bougainvillaea have found a way of demonstrating their grace to the passer-by. Often you don't notice; they might twine themselves in your hair

as you walk by, or else bring you up with their perfume. Astonished, you turn your head , and they in turn bend over the top of the wall like dark-haired young girls and greet you.

Each step you take changes the view. It is never straight, never monotonous. Some doors are arched, others rectangular, with dates and monograms carved on their lintels, each emphasising its own presence. And further up, or else alongside, the windows seem like eyes looking out at the world and gathering the light. The house roofs, flat for the most part, some higher, some lower, allow the dome or bell tower of a church to emerge gracefully. And amongst all these multiple levels a small chimney is coupled with its neighbour, half-hidden by the tiled roof of some mansion. A half-open door leading into a flowered courtyard is an ever-present temptation. Never could such simple things, a pot of flowers on a windowsill or by a door, a vine, a humble garden with two or three trees, have forced you to take note of them were it not that in their simplicity and smallness, they form a harmonious relationship of colours and forms. Green by terra-cotta, yellow alongside blue, red on grey-green leaves. And then, dozens of tones and glimmers in the rays of the sun breaking through the foliage. The smell of the earth, watered drop by precious drop, mixed with the odours of basil and carnation, of citrus and jasmine, give the impression of a familiar atmosphere, one which you had forgotten in the city's commonplace greyness.

In your wanderings you won't come across that deceitful and flashy cosmopolitan luxury which takes you away from human measure. Rich or poor, houses show their true face. If at one point your eye stops on the heavy door of a mansion with marble staircases and wrought-iron grilles, it alights next on another, humble and worn by time, with a simple latch protecting a similar dignity. Dignity. A word, archontia, which cannot be expressed in any other language, which can never carry precisely the same overtones as it carries in the world of the islands. It applies to the rich man and the lord, but can just as accurately describe the poor labourer and his wife. Its meaning is neither solely economic, nor social, but rather ethical. You will be told, "come into our archontiko that we may welcome you". And the archontiko will prove to be no mansion, but rather a simple house in which everything is in its proper place in such a way as to confirm at every moment the humanity and dignity of those who live there and of those welcomed.

The owner of a shop standing before his doorway with a smile welcomes you. Your presence is a matter of importance. Customer or friend, it is all one. The profit is shared. The shop is full of a hundred and one things, looking more like a stage set than consumer merchandise. The objects are what they are, and are used for what they were designed for. The colourful packaging, the strange letters, Greek and foreign, which often the shopkeeper cannot even pronounce, the advertising with its photographs, all lose their commercial purpose and become elements in the shop's scenery. A scenery which turns commercial transactions to human relationships.

Passing through a neighbourhood gives you the opportunity of understanding the language of glances. If you think that all around you are indifferent to your presence, you are mistaken. You are a new face, which, even if only for a few minutes, will play an original role in the street's daily performance. A curtain half-opens in a window, and you are watched curiously but discreetly. Who's that? Is he familiar? A stranger? What news does he bring? Where is he going? These are all questions which in essence represent nostalgia for some absent loved one. Two boys leave their play and with staring eyes examine you as though you had something to give them, something to tell them. A girl has overcome her shyness and looks you in the eyes without wishing to hide a passing thought, wanting to tell you proudly: This is my country, see how beautiful it is. Automatically, you understand what your own role is in this small drama: you are the stranger, who becomes a friend and familiar with a simple smile, a kindly glance. The wind, which blows almost constantly and makes the trees bend over the earth; the sun, which casts its arrows at you mercilessly, wherever you may stand; the sea, now restless and now calm, with its thin veil of briny mist on the far edge of the horizon; the earth, strewn with stones, thorns and weeds; all guide your thoughts into new channels. The desire to fly into the heavens, into infinity, with the wind's breath is unquenchable. Is this not how Ikarus was seduced? Was this not the home of the winged sirens who enchanted sailors with their song? Was it not near here that the god Helios, the sun, let his oxen graze unheeded? With eyes half-closed against the strong light, you lose yourself in the world of

myth. You wander in the palace of betrayed Ariadne; as a Minoan boatswain you count the jars of olive oil as they are loaded on board in the still unsubmerged harbour of Santorini; you travel to Limnos as a warrior and rower in Jason's Argo; you sail as a pilgrim to Delos or as a healer to Kos. You are jealous of Calypso's love, and on the open seas, you strain to hear Arion's song on his dolphin. High up on a mountain, Zeus has placed a cloud. The world is vast and measureless, and man is small. A salamander passes in front of you and runs to hide itself in a wall. It is enough to bring you back. A dry taste of dust and salt on your lips. You hear the earth creak beneath your footsteps. The sun declines slowly, and down by the waterside, sounds are intensified and the evenstar shines alone. You return to where you started from, to today.

The narrow streets of the town fill with people. You mingle in the summer's polyglot crowd. Suddenly everything changes. Pointless chatter, and with glass in hand you listen to a modern dance tune. The smells and smoke from the taverns, the cars and motorcycles, the tourist knickknacks and the bright lights depress you with their ordinariness. Only when you leave behind the artificial lights and walk beneath the starlight, by the sea, only then does your mind remember the girl's smile and your soul remember the noonday sun. That is what you will take away as an eternal memory. It is the finest and most human gift the sea of the archipelago could give you.

Memos Tselikas

Dedicated to

Mr. Marinos

Mrs. Vassiliki

N. Karpodinis

Mrs. Hatzidena

Nikolao Rousso

Mrs. Vangelia

Eleni, Maria

and to all the others

whose presence made

this book more beautiful

Y. D.

Nea Kammeni, Santorini

Amorgos

Koufonissi

Rethymno, Krete

Olympi
Chios

Chora, Serifos

Artemonas
Sifnos

27

los

Folegandros

Kalymnos

Rhodes

32

Chora, Ios

Lindos, Rhodes

33

34

Rhodes

The doors on the street, one opposite the other in a row, single or double-leafed, decorated with wrought iron, look like proud ladies. They have their own charm, with their arches, their stone supporters, their worn doorsteps and their heavy bolts. They carry you back far into the past, to the days when they were bolted, fearfully, at the sound of strange voices. Now, with their wood-work freshly painted, they greet every visitor.

Thirassia

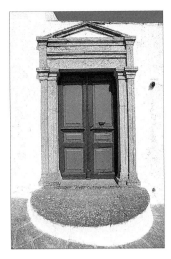  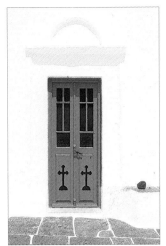

37

Olympos
Karpathos

Fira
Santorini

Koskinou
Rhodes

Skyros

Olympos
Kàrpathos

44

Naoussa, Paros

Ireo, Samos

Naxos

Olympos
Karpathos

Olympos, Karpathos

Oia, Santorini

The straw chairs in the cafes with their wooden braces and the twisted wire between their legs are not made for you to sit and rest. They are so uncomfort- able that you need another on which to rest your feet by the round iron table. And yet they are the only ones which harmonise easily with washed-down cobbles, the smell of coffee and ouzo.

52

53

Mykonos

Kalymnos

Skiathos

Folegandros

Milos

Mykonos

Mykonos

Agiassos, Lesvos

Ano Mera
Mykonos

63

Chios

Olympos, Karpathos

The blue of the sky is the natural, steady

power in the harmony of colours; all the oth-

ers are variables, determined by human taste.

Green, red, ochre, lapis all make up the spec-

trum of daily toil and hope.   The contrasts

and changes across the hull of a fishing ves-

sel or a windowsill against a wall are light

and joyful as the rhythms of island songs.

Kalymnos

69

Parikia
Paros

Stomio

Koufonissi

Milos

Kalymnos

Parikia
Paros

Parikia
Paros

Koufonissi, Keros

Oia
Santorini

Pyrgi, Chios

Olympos, Karpathos

82

Kalymnos

The chapels in the distance stand out like white spots in the green of the vines and the deep golden colour of the harvested fields. Only those which have clambered up into the rocks look like doves about to fly off. Whole armies of white-robed saints remain there, sleepless in their holiness and their solitude beneath the infinity of blue.

Skyros

84

Amorgos

Symi

Telendos, Kalymnos

Santorini

Chryssopigi, Sifnos

91

Rhodes

Mytilini, Lesvos

93

Santorini

Apollon
Naxos

Kastro, Kos

Anavatos, Chios

98

Vatera, Lesvos

The wheel turns thanks to muscle-power or a motor. Like a small god, the potter gives body and form to the amorphous grey mass. The clay, earth from the earth, acquires its soul thanks to the hands and ability of the craftsman. The jugs are earthen bodies, with a neck, hands, belly and mouth. Some are humble and naked, others stand in line, painted and decorated. For centuries now the potter has mirrored the world on their bodies.

Vathy, Sifnos

Fira
Santorini

104

Rethymno, Krete

Mykonos

Mykonos

Kalymnos

Folegandros

110

Merovingli, Santorini

Santorini

113

There are also certain animals, meek and domesticated, which without intending to become of interest, attract your attention. You can still see horses trudging around a threshing-floor, since the property of the farmers is limited, and machines would be too ambitious for small fields. Donkeys and mules are however an essential complement to the landscape, whether carrying vegetables or tourists. As for cats and dogs, they enjoy both the sun and the leavings of the tables.

Olympi, Chios

116

Skopelos

Olympos, Karpathos

Parikia, Paros

121

Oia, Santorini

Medieval City
Rhodes

Koufonissi

125

Oia
Santorini

127

Chora, Amorgos

Parikia, Paros

129

130

Mykonos

Diagonal lines, lines vertical and horizontal, the sharp shapes of the shadows of white walls and stairways. However you struggle to work out their mathematical relationships, the effort is wasted. There is always an unknown factor. It is the turning of the sun, for when it starts to sink into the west, the shadows grow sweeter, the lines relax, embrace and are lost in the infinity of night.

Apollonia
Sifnos

133

Olympos
Karpathos

Serifos

Lesvos

Patmos

Skopelos

Chóra, Serifos

Patmos

Plomari
Lesvos

Kos

Monastery Myrsinidiou,
Chios

Monastery Chosoviotissa,
Amorgos

To those used to living on islands, stair-

ways are a part of life. Their proportions

and symmetry regulate breath and reduce

labour.   Made of stone, whitewashed,

they tie together the most secret corners

of every neighbourhood.   Once upon a

time children would carve ships, flow-

ers, their names and the sun upon them.

Artemonas
Sifnos

Plaka
Leonidi

152

Symi

Chania, Krete

Olympos, Karpathos

Samos

155

Paros

Koufonissi

Kefalos, Kos

Joulis, Kea

159

Mykonos

Oia, Santorini

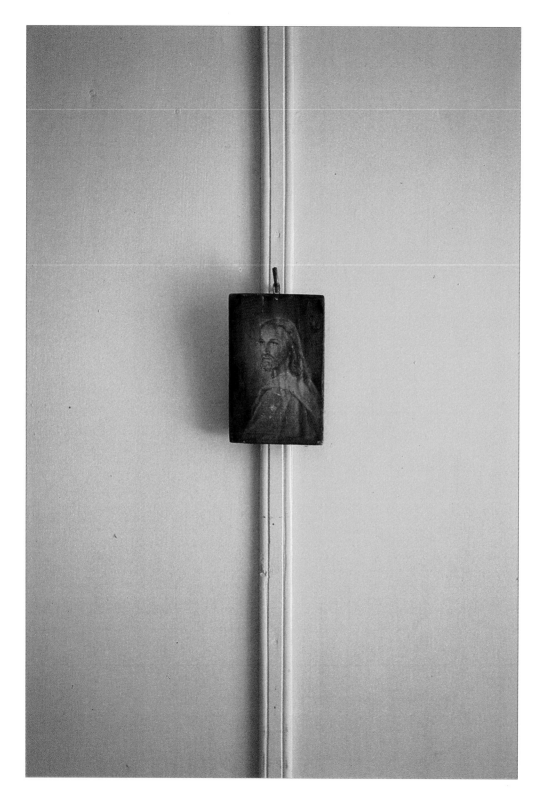

Symi

Olympos
Karpathos

163

164

A pot of basil, two carnations or a gerani-

um are the first things to wish you a good

morning. It doesn't matter whether they

are growing in tins or earthenware pots,

at the very edge of the courtyard or on a

windowsill. The daily watering becomes a

ceremony of greeting to colour and smell.

166

Oia
Santorini

Santorini, 1979

169

Kreta

170

Keros

171

Sifnos

Mykonos

Santorini

Mesta, Chios

176

Artemonas
Sifnos

177

178

Oia, Santorini

Koufonissi

Delos

Symi

Santorini

Serifos

183

184

Sifnos

Santorini

186

INDEX OF PHOTOGRAPHS

Colour Reproductions by
Nikos Alexiades of TOXO Co.
Printing by Haidemenos S.A.
Binding by I.Mantis & Sons Co.

NIKON
cameras and lenses were used
in all of the photographs.